A Seminar Work

Presented By:

Md. Mostafizur Rahman

Lecturer

Department of English Language & Literature

University of Science & Technology Chittagong, USTC.

For Correspondence: Md. Mostafizur Rahman, Lecturer,
Department of English Language & Literature, University of Science
& Technology Chittagong, USTC, email:
lecturer_english_ustc@rahmanmostafiz.com, web:
<http://www.rahmanmostafiz.com>

Sponsored By:

University of Science & Technology Chittagong, USTC.

Organized By:

Department of English Language & Literature

University of Science & Technology Chittagong, USTC.

Source of Inspiration:

A.I. Islam Mr.

Chairman, Janasheba Foundation
&
Director (General Affairs)
University of Science & Technology Chittagong,
USTC.

For Correspondence: Md. Mostafizur Rahman, Lecturer, Department of English Language & Literature, University of Science & Technology Chittagong, USTC, email: lecturer_english_ustc@rahmanmostafiz.com, web: <http://www.rahmanmostafiz.com>

Title:

"An Exploration of Cultural Healing in Derek Walcott's *Omeros*, a Hallmark of Modern Polyglossic Epic."

For Correspondence: Md. Mostafizur Rahman, Lecturer, Department of English Language & Literature, University of Science & Technology Chittagong, USTC, email: lecturer_english_ustc@rahmanmostafiz.com, web: <http://www.rahmanmostafiz.com>

Key Words:

Postcolonial Literature, Derek Walcott, Classical Epic in Modern Period, Multi-vocal Literature, Caribbean Literature.

For Correspondence: Md. Mostafizur Rahman, Lecturer, Department of English Language & Literature, University of Science & Technology Chittagong, USTC, email: lecturer_english_ustc@rahmanmostafiz.com, web: <http://www.rahmanmostafiz.com>

Abstract:

Emerging from over three hundred years of occidental oppression, the Caribbean people find themselves custodians of a culture inseparably cemented to an imperial history. Despite this oppression, or perhaps because of it, a uniquely West Indian consciousness has emerged, during the last decades of 20th century, which draws Walcott's poetic attention. With a view to curing the wounds of Caribbean culture, he attempts to delineate this West Indian spirit in his most ambitious work *Omeros*. Here he portrays some characters whose acts of healing of others' wounds are actually nothing but symbols of healing the wounds of entire Caribbean culture. For example, Ma Kilman's healing Philoctete is actually a symbolic healing of the entire community (elaborately shown in the main paper). My purpose of writing this paper, however, is to explore the concept of cultural healing in this poem through Walcott's engagement with modernist epic poetry.

While writing this epic, Walcott adopts and transforms elements from Pound's *The Cantos*, Eliot's *The Waste Land* and Crane's *The Bridge*. He uses pseudo-Dantean verse, Sapphic prosody, Homeric sensibility and Virgilian methodology, which do

For Correspondence: Md. Mostafizur Rahman, Lecturer, Department of English Language & Literature, University of Science & Technology Chittagong, USTC, email: lecturer_english_ustc@rahmanmostafiz.com, web: <http://www.rahmanmostafiz.com>

not show his inaptness of aesthetic purity of writing epic, but rather shows his attempt to set a new trend in literary modernism. I have defined this new trend as polyglossic epic which I will demonstrate in this paper.

I have organized my paper into two major issues focusing on the process of redefining the epic, and the process of cultural healing in *Omeros*.

For Correspondence: Md. Mostafizur Rahman, Lecturer, Department of English Language & Literature, University of Science & Technology Chittagong, USTC, email: lecturer_english_ustc@rahmanmostafiz.com, web: <http://www.rahmanmostafiz.com>

Introduction:

Once upon a time it was a very common idea among European scholars and critics that the Africans were incapable of producing epic literature. For example, in surveying the heroic poetry of world literature, C.M. Bowra, in his 1952 study Heroic Poetry, found a serious lack of heroic poetry in Africa (specifically in Uganda and Ethiopia) and he wrote about the African poetry "Though these poems, and many others like them, show a real admiration for active and generous manhood, they come from peoples who have no heroic poetry and have never advanced beyond panegyric and lament. The intellectual effort required for such an advance seems to have been beyond their powers."[1] But it is Derek Walcott who has caused the tide to turn and has broken all Eurocentric scholars' and critics' humiliating impressions upon African/Caribbean poets and writers by his ironic handling of the generic conventions of classical epic poetry in *Omeros*.

For Correspondence: Md. Mostafizur Rahman, Lecturer, Department of English Language & Literature, University of Science & Technology Chittagong, USTC, email: lecturer_english_ustc@rahmanmostafiz.com, web: <http://www.rahmanmostafiz.com>

Omeros: a Polyglossic Epic:

Derek Walcott remakes and initiates a new epic tradition in literary modernism. He adapts Dante's three-verse stanzas and thematic frame of the quest for paradise. Walcott has fabricated his most precious work *Omeros* in seven Books, totaling 64 chapters, of three sections each. The verse form of *Omeros* is carefully constructed. Walcott has chosen to craft this ostensibly Caribbean poem in hexametric terza rima[2], one of the most cherished forms of the European literary tradition, and arguably the very foundation upon which the culture of Christian empire was built. This, sometimes, may draw critics' negative impressions about Walcott as terza rima has rarely been able to exploit any sort of nuance whatsoever including the nuances of West Indian culture. But Walcott had a greater intention of choosing terza rima. His intention was to make the readers' minds intertwined into a vast intertexual web of expectations and concerns. A closer inspection of *Omeros* proves that despite most lines' having twelve syllables each, the wildly varied metrical construction of the poem gives the appearance of being

For Correspondence: Md. Mostafizur Rahman, Lecturer, Department of English Language & Literature, University of Science & Technology Chittagong, USTC, email: lecturer_english_ustc@rahmanmostafiz.com, web: <http://www.rahmanmostafiz.com>

free verse. The free verse, incorporating four, five and six beat lines in both stress verse and syllable stress verse, has made this poem an ultimate work of rich prosody which is most unlike anything else ever attempted in English, and is sometimes found in Horace's works with Sapphic prosody. This masterly creation, however, is Walcott's greatness that opens a new gate for us to consider *Omeros* an epic of the new tradition.

In spite of adopting Homeric sensibility in his art of characterization in *Omeros*, Walcott has brought no intervention of Homeric gods and goddesses in this epic. He evokes the rituals of many peoples, from Africa and Europe, North America and the West Indies. In Book- II, Sec- iii, of *Omeros*, the priest blesses the fishermen's canoes and at the same time smiles mockingly when Achille spells faulty English in naming his canoe "In God We Troust"[*]. It shows the book's framework of the imposition of Christianity on Caribbean culture by the European colonizers. Then we see that Maud Plunkett, an Irish and Catholic, attends the local church. Ma Kilman,

For Correspondence: Md. Mostafizur Rahman, Lecturer, Department of English Language & Literature, University of Science & Technology Chittagong, USTC, email: lecturer_english_ustc@rahmanmostafiz.com, web: <http://www.rahmanmostafiz.com>

whose religious inclination is a bridge between Christian and non-Christian religion, also goes to the Catholic Church. Her visiting Catholic church evokes the classical tradition:

"… They called her Ma Kilman

because the village was darkened by their belief

in her as a gardeuse, sybil, obeah-woman

webbed with a spider's knowledge of an after-life

in her cracked lenses. She took Holy Communion

with Maud sometimes, but there was an old African

doubt that paused before taking the wafer's white leaf."[*]

The absence of Homeric gods and goddesses may be a factor for critics to reject *Omeros* as an epic. But Walcott's intentional omitting of those gods and goddesses

For Correspondence: Md. Mostafizur Rahman, Lecturer, Department of English Language & Literature, University of Science & Technology Chittagong, USTC, email: lecturer_english_ustc@rahmanmostafiz.com, web: <http://www.rahmanmostafiz.com>

from this poem never diverts it from the epic tradition. Rather his fabrication of multi-religious ritual performances into the characters having different beliefs and dogmas has a purpose of presenting religious wounds pestering the Caribbean islands, with a view to healing them. This wider and noble purpose has created an obvious notion about *Omeros* as an epic. It is because one of the most vital characteristics of an epic is to represent a poet's attempt to produce an aesthetic intercession on behalf of an entire community or nation.

Language is always a motivating force to form culture, and vice versa. Mara Sanclon in one of her articles has found such an inseparable interrelation between language and culture, "……..the multilingual epic is a cultural production that acts as a national poem for the diverse culture of St. Lucia" (Scanlon, 107) and she strongly argues in the same article that *Omeros* can be called a polyglossic epic as this long poem has its text with poly-vocal language like Creole, Patois[3], Amerindian and so on. Fundamentally, language carries the culture and

For Correspondence: Md. Mostafizur Rahman, Lecturer, Department of English Language & Literature, University of Science & Technology Chittagong, USTC, email: lecturer_english_ustc@rahmanmostafiz.com, web: <http://www.rahmanmostafiz.com>

tradition of a whole nation. It is found by some critics that the West Indians lost their language by a dominating influence of the language of the colonizers. By losing the originality of their language they actually lost their culture. And as Walcott's main motif for writing *Omeros* is cultural healing, which I am going to discuss in the later portion of this paper, he uses a language game to create the full fledged effect of multi-cultural environment. That is to say, polyglossia has been used as a weapon for Walcott to establish his targeted theme in *Omeros* for which I easily can consider this epic a polyglossic one.

The bulk of the epic *Omeros* is written in standard English. But the poem is peppered and penetrated with instances of West Indian dialect and idiom. Let me quote a dialectic utterance of God in this epic;

"Look. **I** giving you permission
to come home. 1s I send the sea-swift as a
pilot,

For Correspondence: Md. Mostafizur Rahman, Lecturer, Department of English Language & Literature, University of Science & Technology Chittagong, USTC, email: lecturer_english_ustc@rahmanmostafiz.com, web: <http://www.rahmanmostafiz.com>

the swift **whose** wings is the sign of my crucifixion.

And thou shalt have no God should in case you forgot

my commandments." [*]

The use of dialectic St. Lucian creole, a recognizably distinct variation of French in *Omeros,* is Walcott's intention to create an environment where one can read them freely without having any sense of etymological ties that bind the Caribbean psyche to the ideology of empire. Because of the intertwined existence of these dialects and local idioms, the entire text of *Omeros* should be analyzed with an awareness of the cadences of St. Lucian speech. Some words are deliberately used by Walcott in this poem with non standard English spelling. Even the names of some characters, taken from the classical epics, are spelled with some significant letters missing from their original spellings. For example, Achille in *Omeros* is a parallel

For Correspondence: Md. Mostafizur Rahman, Lecturer, Department of English Language & Literature, University of Science & Technology Chittagong, USTC, email: lecturer_english_ustc@rahmanmostafiz.com, web: <http://www.rahmanmostafiz.com>

presentation of Homeric hero Achilles. There is a common practice that if a Homeric hero is alluded to, his name must be given its standard spelling. But Walcott deliberately omits 's' from this Homeric hero. A similar case is found in the character Philoctete. His name also is mentioned missing 's', which means that his name has not been given its standard spelling. Though *Omeros*, like all other works of Walcott, is written in standard English, its frequent use of dialects and local idioms create a multi-lingual or polyglossic effect on the entire text of this epic.

In fact, *Omeros* is a decorated platform of multi-lingual culture where apparently there may not be all characteristics of a classical epic. But a research work, as I have presented in my above discussion, can prove Walcott's deliberate deviation from some major characteristics of traditional epic as an attempt at remaking the epic tradition, which I have defined as a polyglossic epic.

For Correspondence: Md. Mostafizur Rahman, Lecturer, Department of English Language & Literature, University of Science & Technology Chittagong, USTC, email: lecturer_english_ustc@rahmanmostafiz.com, web: <http://www.rahmanmostafiz.com>

Healing the Wounds of Caribbean Culture:

Giving voice to the aspirations and values of an entire culture is always a Herculean task. Derek Walcott sets for himself, in *Omeros*, such a mammoth project to heal the wounded Caribbean culture.

Walcott perceives the effect of imperialism in the Caribbean islands which he retroactively manipulates in this epic to construct a general indigenous identity because he conceives indigenization as a necessary component of his project of cultural healing. He is determined not to be complicit in imperialist attitudes and so he foregrounds the repetition of colonial violence in some of the characters' attitudes hoping for poetical redemption from it. He imitates certain elements from the works of Eliot and Crane as they also tried the same. But this imitation does not in any way link it to the imperialistic strain. Rather he seeks to transform and transcend the limitations of their constructions that are linked to imperialism. He has used myths, even in naming the characters, to define indigenous status as a spiritual relation to the existing community

For Correspondence: Md. Mostafizur Rahman, Lecturer, Department of English Language & Literature, University of Science & Technology Chittagong, USTC, email: lecturer_english_ustc@rahmanmostafiz.com, web: <http://www.rahmanmostafiz.com>

rather than to the ancestry which has a history of nothing but colonial impact. Walcott's concept of the sense of indigeneity is actually a process of awakening the individual state of mind which is obviously a part of the process of cultural healing.

A descendant of both the colonizer and the colonized, Walcott provides a poetic vision of Caribbean culture in *Omeros*. He portrays in this epic both Afro-European and Anglo-Caribbean characters with a view to effecting a reconciliation. Each of the main characters is found wounded, visibly or figuratively, followed by ultimate recovery or healing. The heraldic figure Philoctete has a sore on his shin. Major Plankett has an old head-wound and loses his wife; Maud Plunkett suffers from homesickness; Achille suffers from hallucination for traveling back to Africa; and Hector suffers from a zeal of adapting mechanical livelihood. Helen, the symbol of the island of St. Lucia, suffers from an agony of her abandonment by Achille. The narrator also suffers from a wound which he shares with Philoctete. All these wounds

For Correspondence: Md. Mostafizur Rahman, Lecturer, Department of English Language & Literature, University of Science & Technology Chittagong, USTC, email: lecturer_english_ustc@rahmanmostafiz.com, web: <http://www.rahmanmostafiz.com>

show the West Indians' great loss of their cultural identity that are to be healed, as Walcott views and projects in *Omeros*. Johan Ramazani, in his article "The Wound of History", finds Walcott's poetic vision in *Omeros* and says, "The wound in *Omeros* memorializes the untold suffering of Afro-Caribbeans, yet as trope, it inevitably poeticizes pain, compares this particular experience with others, and thus must either mar or deconstruct experiential uniqueness by plunging it into the whirlpool of metaphorical resemblance and difference." (Ramazani, 71).

Healing, in *Omeros*, is handled in various ways. Philoctete is cured by Ma Kilman's herbal treatment, Plunkett is healed by learning how to accept present life forgetting the past history, the narrator is healed by freeing himself from his classical Greek love, Maud Plunkett is healed (symbolic healing) as he dies at last, Hector is also saved by his death, Achille is healed by believing the uniqueness of the beauty of his own village and own woman. Through all these acts of healing, Walcott has

For Correspondence: Md. Mostafizur Rahman, Lecturer, Department of English Language & Literature, University of Science & Technology Chittagong, USTC, email: lecturer_english_ustc@rahmanmostafiz.com, web: <http://www.rahmanmostafiz.com>

planted his poetic vision that I wish to discuss in the next passages in detail.

The epic *Omeros* opens, among some spectacular descriptions of nature, with Philoctet's telling the story of how the people of his island are engaged in cutting down trees to make fishing boats in order to earn their living.

"This is how, one sunrise, we cut down them canoes." [*]

Just after that, Philoctet finds a very dreadful scar on his leg obtained from a rusted anchor while he was pulling his boat onto the shore. Because of this wound he has to limp holding his knee on his one hand. He feels pain not only on one part of the body but also on the whole body which is considered not be cured until his death. This incurable physical pain colonizes Philoctet's whole body in the very same way as the European colonizers colonized the island of St. Lucia. So the healing of this physical

For Correspondence: Md. Mostafizur Rahman, Lecturer, Department of English Language & Literature, University of Science & Technology Chittagong, USTC, email: lecturer_english_ustc@rahmanmostafiz.com, web: <http://www.rahmanmostafiz.com>

wound, discussed in some later passages, will obviously be the healing of the island's wounds and troubles, I believe.

Philoctete's wound makes him a social outcast. It is because the scar spreads a very rough smell into the community he lives in. It prevents his usual living among the people around him which, to me, is the most intolerable suffering a man undergoes. At the very outset of Chapter-I in *Omeros*, the disgusting social effects of the wound are found in the following description:

"………. Soon he would run,

hobbling, to the useless shade of an almond,
              with locked teeth, then wave them off from
the shame
              of his smell, and once more they would leave
him alone

under its leoparding light." [*]

For Correspondence: Md. Mostafizur Rahman, Lecturer, Department of English Language & Literature, University of Science & Technology Chittagong, USTC, email: lecturer_english_ustc@rahmanmostafiz.com, web: <http://www.rahmanmostafiz.com>

The above lines show how physical wound produce problematic effects on a man's smooth and habitual living in the community.

The sense of being isolated from normal human activities creates a psychological affliction in Philoctet. He believes that the scar on his leg, by which he is being afflicted, is a token of his 'ancestral burdens and affliction'[*]. While realizing his wound's lineage from his ancestral slavery, Philoctet makes a reference to that past and his position in it:

"He believed the swelling came from the chained ankles

of his grandfathers. Or else why was there no cure?

that cross he carried was not only the anchor's

but that of his race…"[*]

This realization affects Philoctete's emotion and psychology.

For Correspondence: Md. Mostafizur Rahman, Lecturer, Department of English Language & Literature, University of Science & Technology Chittagong, USTC, email: lecturer_english_ustc@rahmanmostafiz.com, web: <http://www.rahmanmostafiz.com>

However, perceiving his inability to fish for his wound, Philoctet finds solace in the oldest bar in the village 'No Pain Café'[4], owned by Ma Kilman, a 'Sybil' or 'Cassandra' figure obeah woman. Ma Kilman is a mother-healer who promises Philoctet to cure his wounds seeing him in her café. The narrator oversees it and narrates:

"Ma Kilman saw Philoctete hobbling up the street,
so she rose from her corner window, a
flask of white acajou, and a jar of yellow Vaseline,
a small enamel basin of ice. He would wait
in the No Pain Café all day There he would lean
down and anoint the mouth of the sore on the shin."

[*]

Having heard the language of dead ancestors from the ants, Ma Kilman conjures her past memories as to how her grandmother was cured; and she decides to implement that hyper-metaphysical system of healing wounds, which symbolically shows the retrieval of St. Lucia's lost culture.

For Correspondence: Md. Mostafizur Rahman, Lecturer, Department of English Language & Literature, University of Science & Technology Chittagong, USTC, email: lecturer_english_ustc@rahmanmostafiz.com, web: <http://www.rahmanmostafiz.com>

It is, I have to say, Walcott's prime exploration in *Omeros*, and is my project goal as well.

With a maternal desire to comfort the pained St. Lucians, in Chapter XLVIII, Ma Kilman works hard to heal Philoctete's wound by means of Caribbean herbs found in the St. Lucian rainforest. The herbal root is a hybrid plant growing from an African seed, brought by a migrating sea swift, in St. Lucian soil. The healing root is, to me, an autobiographical presentation of Walcott's hybrid identity. The remedial use of this root, so, is Walcott's poetic involvement of himself in healing Caribbean culture, tortured and wounded by the effects of colonial imperialism.

After a while, Ma Kilman backs from the rainforest with the remedial herb and starts working with it to cure Philoctet's scar. Numbering her rosary beads, she recites the name and healing properties of the herb which Baugh sees as a symbol of invoking her ancestral gods, "She goes

For Correspondence: Md. Mostafizur Rahman, Lecturer, Department of English Language & Literature, University of Science & Technology Chittagong, USTC, email: lecturer_english_ustc@rahmanmostafiz.com, web: <http://www.rahmanmostafiz.com>

back behind and beyond Christianity to reaffirm the suppressed or half-forgotten African gods"(Baugh193). She, then, tells Philoctet to have a bath into a long abandoned sugar-mill cauldron used on the slave plantation. At first Philoctet finds himself unwilling to take bath in this cauldron, filled with sea water and the hybrid root. But he surrenders, just within a moment, when he feels the extremity of the agony caused by his festering shin. And so he is bathed, anyway.

"She bathed him in the brew of the root. The basin

was one of those cauldrons from the old sugar-mill,

with its charred pillars, rock pastures, and one gazing." [*]

This is how Philoctet's wound has been cured. With gradual development of the plot of this epic, all other wounds are also found healed. The figurative wound of the transmigrated character Achille, a primary protagonist

For Correspondence: Md. Mostafizur Rahman, Lecturer, Department of English Language & Literature, University of Science & Technology Chittagong, USTC, email: lecturer_english_ustc@rahmanmostafiz.com, web: <http://www.rahmanmostafiz.com>

among the villagers of St. Lucia, is cured only when he realizes that he has to revive a consciousness of his cultural identity. His consciousness has been lost by the influence of British patronization. Achille showed his bravery while helping his British masters in the war against France, as a reward for which bravery he was renamed Achille. After being transformed from Afolable to Achile, he is unable to remember the origin of his identity, as shown in his later conversation with his father Afolable,

> "Everything was forgotten. You also. I do not know.
>
> the deaf sea has changed around every name that you gave
>
> us; trees, men, we yearn for a sound that is missing." [*]

This shows a very significant incident in *Omeros* by which Derek Walcott projects the loss of people's own identity in the Caribbean islands by the influence of

For Correspondence: Md. Mostafizur Rahman, Lecturer, Department of English Language & Literature, University of Science & Technology Chittagong, USTC, email: lecturer_english_ustc@rahmanmostafiz.com, web: <http://www.rahmanmostafiz.com>

Eurocentric imperialism. He then displays a cinematic recovery of that loss by arranging Achille's imaginative journey to Africa and to the sea-bottom.

Achille's epic journey, starts with his fellow fishermen on a fishing boat following the sea swift toward Africa. This happens after a sudden sunstroke delirium on him. In his hallucination, he can see the whole world as well as he sees the present sea where his father and other slaves were drowned or fell dead while being transported from Africa to the Caribbean islands. And so he finds his original home in this sea just under the canoe[5] in which he is being carried. However, Achille's symbolic journey reaches him to Africa where he finds his father and that gives both of them ultimate joy. They find themselves in a conversation while walking through the village. But the languages they use are not the same, as Achille remained absent from Africa for a long time. Talking and walking together of these two individuals of two generations and of two different cultures is overseen by the narrator who

For Correspondence: Md. Mostafizur Rahman, Lecturer, Department of English Language & Literature, University of Science & Technology Chittagong, USTC, email: lecturer_english_ustc@rahmanmostafiz.com, web: <http://www.rahmanmostafiz.com>

regards it as a confrontation between the past and the present:

"two worlds mirrored there

....

and Time stood between them," [*]

Derek Walcott creates this confrontation for linking the present history to that of the past on a new platform. This new platform, which Walcott dreams of for reshaping the lost identity and culture, is a synthesis.

In the very next scene Achille is found in a second subconscious hallucination when we see him on the bed in his home, though it is also an imaginary presence in Africa. In this subconscious state of his hallucination, created by drinking alcohol, he travels to the bottom of the sea where he walked for three hundred years,

"walked the ribbed sand under the flat keels of whales" [*]

For Correspondence: Md. Mostafizur Rahman, Lecturer, Department of English Language & Literature, University of Science & Technology Chittagong, USTC, email: lecturer_english_ustc@rahmanmostafiz.com, web: <http://www.rahmanmostafiz.com>

In this imaginary submersion, he sees there a series of graves of his ancestors among whom he finds his own shadow. In the river in Africa, he also sees a reflection of his canoe. If the canoe symbolizes the Caribbean culture, then this dreamy reflection is nothing but a figurative wound in Achille for which he is not able to find the existence of present Caribbean culture in the past history, as Africa is an abode of his ancestry. The journey leads him to a conclusion that nowhere he can find complete history of his happy existence except in the sea, the Black Atlantic[6], where the present and the past are mingled to form a new consciousness in his mind. This consciousness, built in his dream, comes into his reality just after his hallucination's being broken by the screams of Helen in the form of Circe[7],

"Then Circe embraced her swine" [*]

This is how Achille's figurative wounds are cured by a figurative journey to Africa and a figurative coming

For Correspondence: Md. Mostafizur Rahman, Lecturer, Department of English Language & Literature, University of Science & Technology Chittagong, USTC, email: lecturer_english_ustc@rahmanmostafiz.com, web: <http://www.rahmanmostafiz.com>

back to St. Lucia, regaining his lost Helen. I am sure that Walcott spares no pains to create this transmigrated character's epic journey with a view to establishing his *Omeros* as a successful enterprise for healing the wounds of Caribbean culture.

Achille's competitor, in the battle of winning Helen, Hector is found wounded with jealousy, an instigating passion for a man to be destroyed ultimately. Hector appears first in the opening scene of Cahpter-II, Book-I, with a ceremonial thanks to the sea as the sea is the main source of livelihood for the people of the island. In Chapter-III, of the same book he is found on the fishing boat tearing Achille's shirt. It shows his extreme anger, arousing from the issue of winning Helen by Achille, which leads these two fishermen to an unsettled battle, a battle that echoes Hellenic war in classical epics.

"The duel of these fishermen

was over a shadow and its name was Helen"

[*]

For Correspondence: Md. Mostafizur Rahman, Lecturer, Department of English Language & Literature, University of Science & Technology Chittagong, USTC, email: lecturer_english_ustc@rahmanmostafiz.com, web: <http://www.rahmanmostafiz.com>

In a following scene Hector, along with his canoe, is taken far away from the shore and he comes, after a desperate struggle with nature, back to the shore. The loss of his canoe results him buying a taxi called 'comet'[8], a symbolic adaptation of imperialism in him. Hoping piles of money, Hector alienates himself from his original tradition and invites modernism in his life. His comet is, to me, an Icarian kite, riding on which seems a space travel for which old women of the island regard it as a hell,

"Hell? Already?" [*]

But Helen is fascinated with this modern adaptation and rides on this comet which shows a psychological change that makes St. Lucians facing generation gap, an obvious cultural wound, I believe. However, Hector drives his taxi recklessly, as if he is running from the truth. While he is driving along a steeply road, a piglet appears to be fallen under the stroke of his taxi and he swerves instantly to save it. But ultimately the comet crashes and Hector dies

For Correspondence: Md. Mostafizur Rahman, Lecturer, Department of English Language & Literature, University of Science & Technology Chittagong, USTC, email: lecturer_english_ustc@rahmanmostafiz.com, web: <http://www.rahmanmostafiz.com>

on the spot. His dead body is taken nearer to the sea for funeral and is engraved there. Hector finds his peaceful home. All his relentless effort for earning more money ends. He is once again loved by his fellow fishermen, even by his ever rival Achille. Honouring previous friendship, Achille wishes Hector,

"Sleep good. Good night"[*]

This is how Hector is saved, though at the cost of his life, as if the whole island's wounds have been healed which is what Walcott's epic projection in *Omeros* is.

Now let me explore what Walcott projects in the character of Helen, another transmigrated character whose beauty fascinates all heraldic figures in *Omeros*. Verily like Homeric Helen, the Carribean Helen is also presented as an icon of beauty. She is compared to a wild and untamed panther, with deadly feline grace. Her beauty mesmerizes those, people of the island as well as the tourists, who watch her. But it is the basic problem with

For Correspondence: Md. Mostafizur Rahman, Lecturer, Department of English Language & Literature, University of Science & Technology Chittagong, USTC, email: lecturer_english_ustc@rahmanmostafiz.com, web: <http://www.rahmanmostafiz.com>

this character that influence of money changes her attitudes, as Achille says,

"Money will change her" [*]

Helen is the embodiment of St. Lucia. So, money-mattering shifts in her attitudes show significant changes in the island mounted by the influence of colonizing economy, which, I must say, is a wound trope in *Omeros* that Walcott presents for recovery.

Unlike Homeric one, Helen in *Omeros* is found serving the Plunkett family where she acts as a maid at the same time as a mistress to Dennis Plunkett, for which, and also for her living with Hector, she is addressed as a whore by Achille,

"More men plough that body than canoe plough the sea" [*]

For Correspondence: Md. Mostafizur Rahman, Lecturer, Department of English Language & Literature, University of Science & Technology Chittagong, USTC, email: lecturer_english_ustc@rahmanmostafiz.com, web: <http://www.rahmanmostafiz.com>

Derek Walcott has used this sex imagery for showing a significant wound in the island of St. Lucia that it has lost its virginity by the impact of colonization. Helen's opening her sexual limbs for Plunkett, so, is the island's absorbing colonizers' culture that causes the ultimate afflictions to that of its own. However, Helen is found pregnant but she can not identify the man who caused it, though it is identified by Ma Kilman as Hector's. Being pregnant and out of work she appears before Maud Plunkett for financial help. But rejection by Maud makes her grievous. Her grief mounts to the peak when Hector dies. Death of Hector brings Helen to Achille closer. After completing Hector's funeral, Achille takes up Hector's bailing tin with Helen's permission. Helen grieves herself thinking that the rites of life in the island is still going on unchanged. It shows the beginning of Helen's self recovery followed by a next scene, in chapter LIII, where she is found more cured,

"I coming home"[*]

For Correspondence: Md. Mostafizur Rahman, Lecturer, Department of English Language & Literature, University of Science & Technology Chittagong, USTC, email: lecturer_english_ustc@rahmanmostafiz.com, web: <http://www.rahmanmostafiz.com>

This is how Helen, finding no alternative way of happiness except exploring her own self, goes to Achille finally. It is a symbolic homecoming and reunion of Homeric Helen with Menelaus by which Walcott demonstrates a synthesis of his *Omeros* project; and that is obviously, I believe, a healing of St. Lucia's loss of culture and identity.

In fact, healing of all these wounds, as I have explored and discussed in this paper, brings a new beginning to the lives of the Caribbean people presented in *Omeros*. People, as well as the poet narrator himself, are now thinking themselves relieved of what they were wounded with. Achille is shown crying, out of ultimate happiness, in the rain. Helen is found spending happy moments with Achille in the garden. The garden is described by the narrator as the Garden of Eden. No malevolent forces are found in the island as if Walcott has washed his hybrid home St. Lucia with the stream of his poetic vision employed in *Omeros*.

For Correspondence: Md. Mostafizur Rahman, Lecturer, Department of English Language & Literature, University of Science & Technology Chittagong, USTC, email: lecturer_english_ustc@rahmanmostafiz.com, web: <http://www.rahmanmostafiz.com>

Notes and References:

. The asterisk '' mark refers to the electronic text of "Walcott, Derek. *Omeros*. New York: Farrar, Straus and Giroux, 1990." Purchased from <http://www.amazon.com/Omeros- Derek-Walcott/dp/0374523509/>

1. Bowra, C. M. *Heroic Poetry*. London: Macmillan, 1952.

2. The literal translation of terza rima from Italian is 'third rhyme'. Terza rima is a three-line stanza using chain rhyme in the pattern A-B-A, B-C-B, C-D-C, D-E-D. There is no limit to the number of lines, but poems or sections of poems written in terza rima end with either a single line or couplet repeating the rhyme of the middle line of the final tercet. The two possible endings for the example above are d-e-d, e or d-e-d, e-e. There is no set rhythm for terza rima, but in English, iambic pentameter is generally preferred.The first known use of terza rima is in Dante's *Divina Commedia*.

   Source: <http://en.wikipedia.org/wiki/Terza_rima>.

3. Patois is French Creole in the Caribbean; especially in Dominica, St. Lucia, Trinidad and Tobago & Haiti).

   Source: <http://en.wiktionary.org/wiki/patois>.

4. A drinking bar owned and maintained by Ma Kilman.

For Correspondence: Md. Mostafizur Rahman, Lecturer, Department of English Language & Literature, University of Science & Technology Chittagong, USTC, email: lecturer_english_ustc@rahmanmostafiz.com, web: <http://www.rahmanmostafiz.com>

5. A **canoe** is a lightweight narrow boat, typically pointed at both ends and open on top, propelled by one or more seated or kneeling paddlers facing the direction of travel using a single-bladed paddle.
Source: <http://en.wikipedia.org/wiki/canoe >.

6. Gilory Paul. *The Black Atlantic: Modernity and Double Consciousness*. Harvard University Press, 1995.

7. In Greek mythology, **Circe** was renowned for her vast knowledge of drugs and herbs. Through the use of magical potions and a wand she transformed her enemies, or those who offended her, into animals. She was a minor goddess of magic. By most accounts, Circe was the daughter of Helios, the god of the sun, and Perse, an Oceanid.
Source: <http://en.wikipedia.org/wiki/circe>.

8. Name of the taxi that Hector bought in order to earn more money.

Bibliography:

1. Walcott, Derek. *Omeros*. New York: Farrar, Straus and Giroux, 1990.

For Correspondence: Md. Mostafizur Rahman, Lecturer, Department of English Language & Literature, University of Science & Technology Chittagong, USTC, email: lecturer_english_ustc@rahmanmostafiz.com, web: <http://www.rahmanmostafiz.com>

2. Bloom, Harold. *The Anxiety of Influence: A Theory of Poetry*. London, Oxford, and New York: Oxford University Press, 1973.

3. Leckie, William H. *The Buffalo Soldiers: A Narrative of the Negro Cavalry in the West. Norman*: University of Oklahoma Press, 1967.

4. Lado, Robert. *Linguistics Across Cultures*. Ann Arbor: University of Michigan Press, 1957.

5. Habekost, Christian . *Verbal Riddim: The Politics and Aesthetics of African-Caribbean Dub Poetry*. Amsterdam: Rodopi, 1 993.

6. Mohammed, El sheikh. *Colonial and Postcolonial Literature*. New York: Oxford UP, 1995.

7. Hamner, Robert Daniel. *Epic of the Dispossessed: Derek Walcott's Omeros*. Columbia and London: University of Missouri Press, 1997.

8. Baugh, Edward: *Derek Walcott*. Cambridge University Press, 2006.

9. Bhabha, Homi K. *The Location of Culture*. London: Routledge, 1994.

10. Breslin, Paul. *Nobody's Nation: Reading Derek Walcott*. Chicago: University of Chicago, 2001.

11. Burnett, Paula. *Derek Walcott: Politics and Poetics*. Gainesville, Fl.: U of Florida P, 2000.

For Correspondence: Md. Mostafizur Rahman, Lecturer, Department of English Language & Literature, University of Science & Technology Chittagong, USTC, email: lecturer_english_ustc@rahmanmostafiz.com, web: <http://www.rahmanmostafiz.com>

12. Scanlon, Mara. "'In the Mouths of the Tribe': 'Omeros' and the Heteroglossic Nation" *Bakhtin and the Nation*. Lewisburg, PA: Bucknell University Press, 2000: 101-117.

13. Lucie-Smith, Edward. "West Indian Writing" *The London Magazine* 8.4 (1968): 96-102.

14. Steiner, George. "From Caxton to Omeros" *Times Literary Supplement* 27 (1993): 13-16.

15. Ramazani, Jahan. "The Wound of History: Walcott's Omeros and the Postcolonial Poetics of Afliction." *Publications of the Modern Language Association of America* 1123 (1997): 405.

16. Figueroa, Victor. "Encomium of Helen: Derek Walcott's Ethical Twist in 'Omeros'". *Twentieth Century Literature*. Spring 53:1 (2007): 23-39.

17. Collins, Loretta. "We Shall all Heal: Ma Kilman, the Obeah-woman, as Mother-Healer in Derek Walcott's Omeros." *Literature and Medicine* (1995): 14.1, 146-62.

18. Davis, Gregson. "With No Homeric Shadow: The Disavowal of Epic in Derek Walcott's Omeros." *South Atlantic Quarterly* 96.2 (1997): 321-33.

19. Van Sickle, John B., 'The Design of Derek Walcott's Omeros'. *Classical World*, 93:1 (1999): 7-27.

20. Lernout, Geert. "Derek Walcott's Omeros: The Isle is Full of Voices." *Kunapipi* 14.2 (1992): 90-104.

For Correspondence: Md. Mostafizur Rahman, Lecturer, Department of English Language & Literature, University of Science & Technology Chittagong, USTC, email: lecturer_english_ustc@rahmanmostafiz.com, web: <http://www.rahmanmostafiz.com>

Online References:

1. <http://www.amazon.com/Omeros-Derek-Walcott/dp/0374523509/>

2. <http://www.123helpme.com/>

3. <http://dictionary.cambridge.org/>

4. <http://www.oxfordreference.com/>

5. <http://www.online-literature.com/>

6. <http://www.openculture.com/free_ebooks/>

7. <http://www.bibliomania.com/>

8. <http://www.bookboon.com/>

9. <http://www.digilibraries.com/>

10. <http://www.p-books.com/>

11. <http://www.gutenberg.org/>

For Correspondence: Md. Mostafizur Rahman, Lecturer, Department of English Language & Literature, University of Science & Technology Chittagong, USTC, email: lecturer_english_ustc@rahmanmostafiz.com, web: <http://www.rahmanmostafiz.com>

CPSIA information can be obtained
at www.ICGtesting.com
Printed in the USA
LVHW080133310522
720082LV00011B/624